UNIVERSITY OF MINNESOTA

F. Scott Fitzgerald

BY CHARLES E. SHAIN

UNIVERSITY OF MINNESOTA PRESS · MINNEAPOLIS

F. SCOTT FITZGERALD

CHARLES E. SHAIN is a professor of English and member of the American Studies faculty at Carleton College, Northfield, Minnesota. He has contributed articles to various journals.

⩘ F. Scott Fitzgerald

THE general acceptance of Scott Fitzgerald into the ranks of serious and ambitious American novelists had to wait until his death in 1940. He was forty-four when he died and the story of the early rise and abrupt fall of his literary reputation — as well as his personal fortunes — can be fitted with neat symmetry into those two dramatic decades of the American twentieth century, the twenties and the thirties. The twenties were less than three months old when Fitzgerald's first novel, *This Side of Paradise*, arrived and immediately became a famous American book. Within weeks of this first success a second brand-new, postwar product, his stories of the flapper and her boy friends, made it clear that the twenties would be his oyster and that he, handsome, clever, and lucky Scott Fitzgerald, would be one of the brightest figures of the new age. The climax of his fortunes arrived, we can see now, very rapidly. In 1925 came the splendid artistic success of *The Great Gatsby*, and then in the second half of the twenties the days and months of his private world began to descend into tragedy. He could not bring the order into his life that would allow him to write his next novel. By the end of the twenties he was living too high and drinking too much. In April 1930 Zelda Fitzgerald had the mental breakdown that ended the romantic life they had built together over the preceding ten years. During the thirties, his last decade, Fitzgerald's life encompassed enough pathos, irony, and final agony to make his biography by Arthur Mizener one of the saddest records of an American literary life since Edgar

5

Allan Poe. Before he died he was dead as a writer. No one was buying his books though seven were still in print. What has become clearer since his death in 1940 is a final irony, at the expense not of Fitzgerald but of American literary culture: the neglect he suffered during the 1930's was hugely undeserved. It took two posthumously published works to reveal to America how much serious work he had accomplished against great odds during the last ten years of his life.

The critical neglect of Fitzgerald had of course the effect of making the popular neglect seem deserved. That he shortened his own life by dissipation and wasted his fine talent all along the way was the judgment passed by most of the critics at the time of his death. The severity of their judgments may have been justified, but this did not excuse the failure to see how hard Fitzgerald had written all his life, or the failure to distinguish his best work from the rest and to recognize how much good work there was. It will perhaps become less of a temptation as the decades pass to be preoccupied with Fitzgerald as a person, and with his life as a cautionary tale, at the expense of a close concentration on his stories and novels. He used himself so mercilessly in his fiction, there is often such a complete fusion between his life and his stories, that conscientious criticism will always have to remember D. H. Lawrence's warning to biographically-minded critics: don't trust the artist, trust the tale. There is, however, another order of difficulty in appreciating Fitzgerald's best work. His attitude toward money and moneyed people has been much misunderstood.

One way to begin a consideration of Fitzgerald's attraction to the American rich as the prime subject matter of his fiction is to look at the most famous Fitzgerald literary anecdote. As Ernest Hemingway originally wrote it into his story "The Snows of Kilimanjaro," published in *Esquire* in 1936, it went this way. Hemingway's writer-hero is musing on his own life among the

6

American rich. "He remembered poor Scott Fitzgerald and his romantic awe of them and how he had started a story once that began, 'The very rich are different from you and me.' And how someone had said to Scott, Yes they have more money. But that was not humorous to Scott."

Although the exchange never actually took place it has become part of the story of our two most legendary modern novelists. The moral implications of the anecdote, political, personal, and artistic, have usually been chalked up to Hemingway's score. It is significant for understanding the distance that separated the two men at this point in their friendship that Hemingway could make such demeaning use of Fitzgerald as a character in a piece of magazine fiction. The anecdote concludes with this comment, "He thought they were a special glamorous race and when he found they weren't it wrecked him just as much as any other thing that wrecked him." This was the public burial of a has-been writer, and Fitzgerald was deeply offended.

Hemingway's rebuke belongs to the general charge against Fitzgerald made frequently in the thirties that he was captivated by the rich and their expensive manners, and forgot that too much money in America is always supposed to be a sign of vulgarity and wickedness. Applied to Fitzgerald's fiction this moralism is simple-minded. To disprove it there is exhibited in the novels and stories all the moral energy that Fitzgerald spent "fixing" the rich. Since we read Fitzgerald's stories of the rich in a more affluent American society, in which the rich have become less shocking because they are now less removed from middle-class mores, we should more easily detect the moral and cultural confusions in Fitzgerald's fiction if they are really there. Americans living through a new postwar society can no longer feel superior to Fitzgerald's interest in the American greed for fine cars, the right clothes, and the pleasures of the best hotels and off-beat entertainment. The

7

American people now seem to be less embarrassed than they once were at the snobbery of large parts of their social system. Contemporary social analysis has shown them how far ahead of his times Fitzgerald was in describing the rigorous systems of status that underlie that rather contradictory American term, the Open Society.

We may in fact be today more responsive readers of Fitzgerald's stories of money and display and expensive charm than many of his contemporaries were. He wrote during two decades when an American social revolution seemed more probable to thoughtful people than it does today. Nowadays we may be more ready to accept as he did the final complexity of our society and to recognize that we create a large part of our moral selves as we become engaged in that society. This is the theme that runs through his fiction — and through his life. We do him an injustice if we assume at the start that in order to understand the dreadful sanctions of social prestige — that is, money — Fitzgerald had to make a fatal submission of himself to the glamorous rich.

The story of the legendary Fitzgerald of the twenties usually begins with the picture of newly married, handsome Zelda and Scott Fitzgerald dancing around or jumping into the fountain of the Plaza Hotel. This pastoral scene may be useful in reminding us that the Fitzgeralds were not native New Yorkers. She was from the deep South, from Montgomery, Alabama. He was a midwesterner. Edmund Wilson, one of Fitzgerald's closest literary friends, insisted on the important influence of St. Paul, Minnesota, in forming Fitzgerald's literary personality. In 1922 when Wilson did a literary profile of Fitzgerald he wrote, "Fitzgerald is as much of the middle west of large cities and country clubs as Lewis is of the middle west of the prairies and little towns." The culture that formed him, Wilson went on in a superior eastern

8

manner, was characterized at its best by "sensitivity and eager-
ness for life without a sound base of culture and taste; a brilliant
structure of hotels and exhilarating social activities built not on
the eighteenth century but simply on the prairie." Wilson then
took the occasion to advise Fitzgerald — his friends were always
giving him advice in public — to exploit the "vigorous social
atmosphere" of his native state, "to do for Summit Avenue what
Lewis has done for Main Street." Fitzgerald never followed Wilson's suggestion to write a midwestern novel — despite all that
public advice one of Fitzgerald's most surprising attributes was a
capacity for making up his mind in private — but he made his
own kind of use of his Minnesota background. It was not at all
like Sinclair Lewis's exploitation of that same territory.

Francis Scott Key Fitzgerald was born in St. Paul on September
24, 1896. On his mother's side he was the grandson of an Irish
immigrant who did well in the wholesale grocery business. His
grandfather's estate was worth three to four hundred thousand
dollars when he died at the age of forty-four. This McQuillan
money gave young Scott Fitzgerald the advantageous background
of his grandmother's large house on Summit Avenue, the most
aristocratic street in St. Paul, and it gave him eventually his expensive education in private schools and at Princeton. But he
was always sensitive to the McQuillan beginnings as being what
he called "straight 1850 potato famine Irish." The other half of
his inheritance was much more pleasing to his keen sense of himself. His admiration for his gentlemanly but ineffectual father,
who was descended from a seventeenth-century Maryland family,
he put into both *The Great Gatsby* and *Tender Is the Night*. He
was named for Francis Scott Key, a distant cousin of his paternal
grandmother's. In the thirties he wrote that he had early developed
an inferiority complex in the midst of a family where the "black
Irish half . . . had the money and looked down upon the Mary-

9

land side of the family who had, and really had, that . . . series of reticences and obligations that go under the poor old shattered word 'breeding.' "

Fitzgerald's Catholic background was also oppressive to him as a boy. He wrote in his notebook later in his life that when he was young "the boys in my street still thought that Catholics drilled in the cellar every night with the idea of making Pius the Ninth autocrat of this republic." But Fitzgerald never wrote these feelings of social displacement directly into his fiction or into the confessional essays of the mid-thirties. None of his important protagonists is noticeably Irish or Catholic and none of the agonies they suffer is religious. He was not, apparently, a very devout schoolboy, even in a Catholic boarding school and under the influence of a sophisticated and cultivated priest, Monsignor Fay, who was devoted to him and to whom he dedicated his first novel. (*This Side of Paradise* is not at all a Catholic novel.) In 1919 at the end of his college career at Princeton and his war service he wrote to Edmund Wilson that his Catholicism was scarcely more than a memory. The autobiographical essays in *The Crack-Up* tell us a great deal about Fitzgerald's sense of sinning against himself, against his gift of life and his gift of talent, but none of the sources of his despair take us directly back to his early years in the midst of a dubiously genteel Irish Catholic family in St. Paul.

His loyalty to his father may have been partly a way of defending his father against failure in business. As a boy of eleven Fitzgerald shared intensely the embarrassment of his father's being fired as a salesman for Proctor and Gamble in Buffalo and the family's subsequent return to St. Paul to live under the protection of the McQuillan money. As if his family were restive under the pressures of feeling dependent, they moved from one house to another in the Summit Avenue neighborhood, circling the social strongholds but never able to afford more than "a house below the average/Of a street above the average" as Fitzgerald once put it. One of his best known stories, "Winter Dreams," a Jazz Age version of the Horatio Alger fable, is based on St. Paul and its summertime suburb White Bear Lake. The hero at fourteen is a grocer's son who must earn his spending money as a caddy at the country club to which many of Fitzgerald's Summit Avenue friends belonged. Fitzgerald was never a caddy, but it was easy for him to project a poor boy's social insecurity. His mother was a further embarrassment. She dressed oddly and sometimes behaved oddly in public. He was always aware that she had spoiled him and helped him to be the little show-off who could easily get on the nerves of his teachers and contemporaries. But the young Fitzgerald is also remembered in St. Paul as an imaginative, vital, and attractive boy. Plenty of social success came his way before he was sent off to boarding school in New Jersey at the age of fourteen.

Fitzgerald mined his boyhood years, as he did every stage of his life, for story material. The *Saturday Evening Post* stories of his youth in St. Paul and at Newman School that he wrote at the end of the twenties are delightful and show what a competent writer of magazine fiction he was by this time. But the moments in the stories that distinguish them as Fitzgerald's are those that show how exactly he could recall a moment of a boy's deep feeling about a person, or a place, or "the way it was." One of the safest generalizations that can be made about Fitzgerald is that he is America's most sentient novelist of manners. He was deeply interested in recording the history of his own sensibility at the same time that he wanted to describe a typical American boyhood. The *Post* stories of his young hero Basil Duke Lee are full of events that have their meaning in social distinctions, envious comparisons, and the important implications for young Americans of manners and possessions. But as Basil moves from one emotional crisis to another in his search for who he really is and who he wants

11

to be, Fitzgerald would have us believe that Basil deliberately penetrates each moment of passion for its absolute emotional significance, and then passes on. On one magical late summer afternoon in a St. Paul backyard — the story is called "The Scandal Detectives" — fourteen-year-old Basil really looked into a girl's beautiful, "gnome-like" face for the first time. He had scarcely begun to drink his fill of his response to her, "a warm chill of mingled pleasure and pain," when, Fitzgerald writes, he realized it was "a definite experience and he was immediately conscious of it." Then, as the swift moment of excitement filled him to the brim the boy consciously let it go, "incapable of exploiting it until he had digested it alone." The emotional plot of the story is about a writer-to-be, as well as, we are almost persuaded, a typical American boy.

Fitzgerald's first boyish successes were literary and they were important to both his emotional and his social life. In an autobiographical essay written in the mid-thirties he recalled a piece of schoolboy writing and remembered how necessary it had been to his ability to meet the world. At Newman School the football coach had taken him out of a game unfairly, according to Fitzgerald. The coach thought he had been afraid of an opposing player and had let the team down. Fitzgerald was able to dominate the whole situation, the coach, his lack of success at football, and probably his own cowardice by writing a poem about the experience that made his father proud of him. "So when I went home that Christmas vacation it was in my mind that if you weren't able to function in action you might at least be able to tell about it, because you felt the same intensity — it was a back door way out of facing reality." The need to feel the same intensity of social success that more popular, better balanced schoolboys felt kept Fitzgerald writing stories, poems, and plays. His academic record always suffered, but as a young poet, editor, and playwright he could express his considerable ego and win the kind of public acclaim that was necessary to him. By the age of sixteen he had written and produced two melodramas that had public performances in St. Paul and earned over two hundred dollars for a local charity. He was learning to depend on his literary talent very early in his life. When it came time to choose a college he chose Princeton because he learned that you could be a big man at Princeton if you could provide librettos for its musical comedy organization, the Triangle Club. He entered college in the fall of 1913 when he was still sixteen years old.

Princeton's contribution to Fitzgerald's education as an American writer can be best discovered in his autobiographical first novel, *This Side of Paradise*. For the writer as a person it was, from the first moment, a lovely place, an atmosphere full of poignant emotions. ". . . the sense of all the gorgeous youth that has rioted through here in two hundred years" — that was one of the feelings written into the novel, and as Fitzgerald's young men left Princeton for the army camps of World War I they wept for their own lost youth. Through most of the pages of the novel Princeton is primarily a richly complex American social order with very attractive possibilities for a bright young man on the make. The world you aspired to, as soon as you learned your way around, was composed of admirable, even glamorous men, in the classes above you, who could be envied and imitated both for themselves and for their functions in this specialized society. They were the athletes, writers, campus politicians, or just the Men with an Aura. As a freshman you chose your models, entered the intense but secret social competition, and with good luck and much clever management you would be accepted, by the middle of your second year when you joined an eating club, as one of the best of your generation. This was the Princeton that first consumed Fitzgerald's imagination.

What Fitzgerald as an educated man owed to Princeton is harder to discern. Arthur Mizener believes that the group of literary friends that he was lucky to find there — Edmund Wilson and John Peale Bishop were two of them — gave him "the only education he ever got, and, above all, they gave him a respect for literature which was more responsible than anything else for making him a serious man." The narrowness of his educated mind, in one sense the failure of his Princeton education, can be fairly deduced from letters he wrote to his daughter studying at Vassar during the last year of his life.

Twenty-five years after his Princeton career he still recommends what were evidently his own college practices to his daughter. To form a prose style she must read the poets over and over. If she has anything of an ear she will soon hear the difference between poetry and non-poetry and thus have an advantage over most English professors. She must have "some politeness toward ideas," but about adjectives, ". . . all fine prose is based upon the verbs carrying the sentences. . . . Probably the finest technical poem in English is Keats' *Eve of Saint Agnes*. . . . Would you read that poem for me, and report?" Looking back at his own beginnings in college, he identifies himself as a poetic talent. It is the prose talents, he believes, who need the benefits of a formal education; they depend upon "other factors — assimilation of material and careful selection of it, or, more bluntly: having something to say and an interesting, highly developed way of saying it." As for the education of poets, if she will try to give ". . . not the merely *reported* but the *profound* essence of what happened at a prom or after it, perhaps that honesty will come to you — and then you will understand how it is possible to make even a forlorn Laplander *feel* the importance of a trip to Cartier's!"

It was one of the great blows of Fitzgerald's life that his formal Princeton career as he had carefully plotted it and at first began to achieve it was in the end a failure. By the close of his second year

14

he seemed to be well on his way to the first great public display of his personality. He had made the right club, had written the book for a Triangle show, and was an editor of a magazine called *The Tiger.* The aura was beginning to form. But he had overextended himself. Too many academic deficiencies piled up, and under cover of an illness he left college at the beginning of his third year. A year's absence meant forfeiting all the tangible prizes he had aimed for, and he could still relive the pangs of his disappointment twenty years later. When he returned to college in the fall of 1916 he had improved his notion of the superior Princeton type. He began to see more of "literary" men and to fill the literary magazine with his poems and stories. This was the only year of serious education for him at Princeton, and what he learned came chiefly through private reading. He read especially Shaw and Butler and Wells, and read and then imitated Tennyson, Swinburne, and Rupert Brooke. He discovered the prototype for his first hero and novel when he read Compton Mackenzie's *Sinister Street.* Then between his third and fourth years he applied for a commission in the army. What should have been Fitzgerald's last year at Princeton was only two months long and on November 20 he left the campus for Fort Leavenworth.

Before Fitzgerald left Princeton for what was to be fifteen months of service in American training camps — he was never sent overseas — he finished the first of three versions of *This Side of Paradise.* Professor Christian Gauss read the manuscript and returned it saying that it was not ready for publication. During Fitzgerald's first six months as an officer in training he struggled not with army manuals and training exercises but with his manuscript. In the summer of 1918 *The Romantic Egotist*, as he first called the novel, was sent to Scribner's, and in the fall that house rejected it by a vote of two editors to one. Meanwhile he had been transferred to Camp Sheridan near Montgomery, Alabama, and there, on the seventh of September, as he noted precisely in his journal, he fell in love. The girl, barely eighteen, was Zelda Sayre, the daughter of a judge.

The close resemblance between Zelda Sayre — who was going to become Zelda Fitzgerald after a courtship of a year and a half — and the heroines of Fitzgerald's fiction makes it important to try to see her clearly as a person. It is not a simple thing to do. Since her death she has always been referred to unceremoniously as Zelda, even in formal literary essays. But this informality is really a continuing acknowledgment that the combined destinies of Zelda and Scott Fitzgerald are finally one and indivisible. He transmuted their twin biographies into fiction, and we shall probably never find it easy to distinguish between the historical person and Scott Fitzgerald's Zelda.

When Fitzgerald first met Zelda Sayre he was just recovering from the collapse of a college love affair, the central story of his novel in manuscript. The romantic egotist of his novel was free to make another absolute commitment, to invest another beautiful young lady with the aura of "the top girl." (He wrote later into his notebook, "I didn't have the two top things: great animal magnetism or money. I had the two second things, though: good looks and intelligence. So I always got the top girl.") Zelda was beautiful and desirable for herself, but she was also a prize to be won against very worthy competition, all the other presentable young officers in the two army camps near Montgomery. At the moment of triumph when at last he made her his girl we must assume that he felt the same ecstatic joy that filled Jay Gatsby's ineffable moment in the love scene he was going to write five years later. The persons of the drama were the same: the anonymous young lieutenant from the North and the belle of a southern city. The language of the Gatsby passage is as florid and brilliant as anything in modern fiction since Meredith's early novels. "He knew that when he kissed this girl, and forever wed his unutterable visions to her perishable breath, his mind would never romp again like the mind of God. . . . At his lips' touch she blossomed for him like a flower and the incarnation was complete." In *The Great Gatsby* Fitzgerald was in full control of the language of the religion of love spoken by a modern but strangely old-fashioned courtly lover. None of the ironies visited upon Gatsby in the novel is allowed to tarnish his first response to Daisy. The lack of self-consciousness, the commitment to such pure feelings of sexual tenderness and compassion, distinguish Fitzgerald's romantic attitude toward women from any other modern novelist's.

The demands of feeling that Zelda Sayre brought to the courtship and marriage appear to have been as grand in their terms as Fitzgerald's. If we can trust his early descriptions of her in his fiction, she was above all ambitious, like the southern girl in "The Ice Palace" who was planning to live "where things happen on a big scale." And like the flappers in the early stories who baited their elders and showed in all their responses to life that they valued spontaneity and self-expression before those duller virtues that required self-control, Zelda Sayre was daring and had a local reputation for recklessness and unconventionality. She did what she wanted to, and her parents discovered that they belonged to that generation upon whom, as Fitzgerald once wrote in a story, "the great revolution in American family life was to be visited." Her youthful beauty gave her great confidence. The men in her life were expected on the one hand to make gallant gestures, and of these Fitzgerald was quite capable; on the other hand they were expected to promise her a solid and glittering background — here Fitzgerald's lack of expectations after he was discharged from the army in February 1919 sent them both into agonies of frustration.

For four months he struggled in New York to support himself by writing advertising copy by day and to make the fortune that

17

would convince the girl by writing short stories at night. He sold just one story for thirty dollars, and by June he had lost the girl. Zelda broke the engagement. His response to her decision in the summer of 1919 was to chuck his New York job, return to St. Paul, and rewrite his novel. By early September he had finished *This Side of Paradise*, by the middle of the month Scribner's had accepted it, and by early November he had earned over five hundred dollars from three recently written short stories. With the confidence of a real capitalist and the conviction that he had written a best-selling novel, Fitzgerald returned to Montgomery, and there Zelda promised to marry him in the spring when his novel was published.

Fitzgerald did not hold Zelda Sayre morally responsible for the mercenary views she took of their engagement. They both felt poor, and they were both eager to participate in the moneyed society around them. In the United States in 1919, they agreed, the purpose of money was to realize the promises of life. When Gatsby says, in his famous remark, that Daisy's voice sounds like money, we should read him sympathetically enough to understand, as Arthur Mizener has pointed out, that he is not saying that he loves money or that he loves both Daisy and money, but that he loves what the possession of money has done for Daisy's charming voice. And yet after we have said this, we must also say that Daisy Buchanan, because of her money, is seen at last as a false woman and Gatsby as a simple boy from the provinces who has not been able to tell gilt from real gold. The circumstances of the Fitzgeralds' courtship and marriage seem fabulous — in the narrow sense of that word — because they often seem to suggest for us in outline the complex stories of women and marriage and money that Fitzgerald kept returning to in his fiction.

Fitzgerald was as fully aware of the power of women over men as D. H. Lawrence was, but in a different way. In his journal he once made a note that "Men get to be a mixture of the charming mannerisms of the women they have known." In Fitzgerald's fiction the villain has "animal magnetism" and masculinity but in the end he is stupid about women and treats them like whores. The Fitzgerald hero has softer qualities. "His mannerisms were all girls' mannerisms," he noted in plans for what sounds like a characteristic Fitzgerald hero, "rather gentle considerations got from [–] girls, or restrained and made masculine, a trait that, far from being effeminate, gave him a sort of Olympian stature that, in its all-kindness and consideration, was masculine and feminine alike." The men in his fiction are often, as he was, astonished by the fearlessness and recklessness of women. They are also finally made aware of the deceitfulness and moral complacency of many women. Jordan Baker in *The Great Gatsby* and Baby Warren in *Tender Is the Night*, for example, are studies of mercenary American women as dangerous to men as classical sorceresses. Daisy Buchanan and Nicole Warren are fatally irresponsible human beings. All his critics have noticed Fitzgerald's ability to project himself into women's lives. Near the end of his life, when he had decided to see the story of *The Last Tycoon* through the eyes of Cecilia Brady, age twenty-five, he wrote to his editor, "Cecilia is the narrator because I think I know exactly how such a person would react to my story."

To understand Fitzgerald's life and his stories of love and marriage we must be prepared to accept the tragic love plot strongly implied in his biography: he so built himself into Zelda Fitzgerald's life that when in 1930 her life went down, her fall brought him down as well. From Rome during the winter of 1924–25 at the peak of his pleasure over having written *The Great Gatsby*, he wrote to John Peale Bishop: "The cheerfulest things in my life are first Zelda and second the hope that my book has something extraordinary about it. I want to be extravagantly admired again. Zelda and I sometimes indulge in terrible four day rows that always start

19

with a drinking party but we're still enormously in love and about the only truly happily married people I know." This was the Fitzgerald marriage at the height of its turbulent career. In 1933 after Zelda's first severe illness and while they were living quietly and Scott Fitzgerald was making a valiant stand against alcoholism, he characterized their life together in far different terms. "We have a good way of living, basically, for us; we got through a lot and have some way to go; our united front is less a romance than a categorical imperative and when you criticize it in terms of a bum world . . . [it] seems to negate on purpose both past effort and future hope. . . ." The more knowledge we have of the Fitzgeralds' marriage, the less his choice of those strong words "categorical imperative" surprises us. Their married life was a continual source of both the "romance" and the moral education out of which his best fiction came.

The novel with which Fitzgerald won Zelda, *This Side of Paradise,* is usually praised for qualities that pin it closely to an exact moment in American life. Later readers are apt to come to it with the anticipation of an archeologist approaching an interesting ruin. Its publication is always considered to be the event that ushered in the Jazz Age. Glenway Wescott, writing for his and Fitzgerald's generation, said that it had "haunted the decade like a song, popular but perfect." Social historians have pointed out that the college boys of the early twenties really read it. There have been public arguments as to whether or not the petting party first occurred when Fitzgerald's novel said it did or two years earlier. Anyone reading the novel with such interests will not be entirely disappointed. One of the responsibilities it assumes, especially in its first half, is to make the hero, Amory Blaine, report like a cultural spy from inside his generation. "None of the Victorian mothers — and most of the mothers were Victorian — had any idea how casually their daughters were accustomed to be kissed." "The 'belle' had become the 'flirt,' the 'flirt' had become the 'baby vamp.' " "Amory saw girls doing things that even in his memory would have been impossible: eating three-o'clock, after-dance suppers in impossible cafés, talking of every side of life with an air half of earnestness, half of mockery, yet with a furtive excitement that Amory considered stood for a real moral let-down." The "moral let-down" enjoyed by the postwar generation has given the work its reputation for scandal as well as for social realism.

Today, the novel's young libertines, both male and female, would not shock a schoolgirl. Amory Blaine turns out to be a conspicuous moralist who takes the responsibility of kissing very seriously and disapproves of affairs with chorus girls. (He has no scruples, it must be said, against going on a three-week drunk when his girl breaks off their engagement.) At the end of the story he is ennobled by an act of self-sacrifice in an Atlantic City hotel bedroom that no one would admire more than a Victorian mother. For modern readers it is probably better to take for granted the usefulness of *This Side of Paradise* for social historians and to admire from the distance of another age the obviously wholesome morality of the hero. Neither of these is the quality that saves the novel for a later time. What Fitzgerald is really showing is how a young American of his generation discovers what sort of figure he wants to cut, what modes of conduct, gotten out of books as well as out of a keen sense of his contemporaries, he wants to imitate. The flapper and her boy friend do not actually pet behind the closed doors of the smoking room. They talk, and each one says to the other, unconvincingly, "Tell me about yourself. What do you feel?" Meaning, "Tell me about myself. How do I feel?" The real story of *This Side of Paradise* is a report on a young man's emotional readiness for life.

The only interesting morality it presents is the implied morality

21

that comes as a part of his feelings when the hero distinguishes, or fails to distinguish, between an honest and a dishonest emotion. The highly self-conscious purpose of telling Amory Blaine's story was, one suspects, to help Fitzgerald to discover who he really was by looking into the eyes of a girl — there are four girls — or into the mirror of himself that his college contemporaries made. And the wonder of it is that such a self-conscious piece of autobiography could be imagined, presented, and composed as a best-selling novel by a young man of twenty-three.

The novel is very uneven, and full of solemn attempts at abstract thought on literature, war, and socialism. It has vitality and freshness only in moments, and these are always moments of feeling. Fitzgerald said of this first novel many years later, "A lot of people thought it was a fake, and perhaps it was, and a lot of others thought it was a lie, which it was not." It offers the first evidence of Fitzgerald's possession of the gift necessary for a novelist who, like him, writes from so near his own bones, the talent that John Peale Bishop has described as "the rare faculty of being able to experience romantic and ingenuous emotions and a half hour later regard them with satiric detachment." The ingenuous emotions most necessary to the success of *This Side of Paradise* are vanity and all the self-regarding sentiments experienced during first love and the first trials of pride. The satire visited upon them is often as delicate and humorous as in this picture of Amory at a moment of triumphant egoism: "As he put in his studs he realized that he was enjoying life as he would probably never enjoy it again. Everything was hallowed by the haze of his own youth. He had arrived, abreast of the best of his generation at Princeton. He was in love and his love was returned. Turning on all the lights, he looked at himself in the mirror, trying to find in his own face the qualities that made him see more clearly than the great crowd of people, that made him decide firmly, and able to influence and follow his own will. There was little in his life now that he would have changed. . . . Oxford might have been a bigger field."

The ideas in the novel, unlike the tributes paid to a life of feeling, have the foreign country of origin and the importer's labels still on them. Edmund Wilson said *This Side of Paradise* was not really about anything. "Intellectually it amounts to little more than a gesture — a gesture of indefinite revolt." Toward the end of the novel Fitzgerald's normally graceful sentences begin to thicken and "sword-like pioneering personalities, Samuel Butler, Renan and Voltaire," are called in to add the weight of their names to Amory's reflections on the hypocrisy of his elders. The best pages of the novel come early, where Fitzgerald was remembering in marvelous detail the scenes at Newman School and Princeton. Later in his life he would always find it easy to return to those adolescent years, when feelings were all in all. Bishop once accused him of taking seventeen as his norm and believing that after that year life began to fall away from perfection. Fitzgerald replied, "If you make it fifteen I will agree with you."

The Fitzgerald novel, then, began in his acute awareness of a current American style of young life and in his complete willingness to use his own experience as if it were typical. The charm of his first stories and novels is simply the charm of shared vanity and enthusiasm for oneself as an exceptional person. Fitzgerald often persuades us that he was the one sensitive person there — on the country club porch or in a New York street — the first time something happened, or at the very height of the season. And when this ability to exploit his life began to succeed beyond his dreams, the only next step he could think of was to use it harder.

His success arrived almost overnight: 1920 was the *annus mirabilis*. In that year, the *Saturday Evening Post* published six of his stories, *Smart Set* five, and *Scribner's* two. In 1919 he had made

$879 by writing; in 1920 he made $18,850 from his novel, from magazine stories and essays, and from the rights to two stories sold to the movies. His success with the *Saturday Evening Post* and the movies suggests how quickly he had discovered the formulas for popular fiction and the big money. Within fifteen years between 1919 and 1934 Fitzgerald earned, he estimated, four hundred thousand dollars, most of it writing for magazines and the movies. From the beginning of his success Fitzgerald was quite aware of the temptations of commercial writing and how well adapted he was to succumb to them. The question as to whether the conflict between the use and misuse of his talent opened the crack in Fitzgerald's self-respect that at last killed him as a novelist has been argued by many of his friends. Dos Passos spoke at his death for those who thought it did. Fitzgerald had invented for their generation, he said, the writing career based on the popular magazines and he was "tragically destroyed by his own invention."

Fitzgerald's struggle with his literary conscience is often apparent in his letters and journals. He wrote Maxwell Perkins, his editor at Scribner's, that he knew he had "a faculty for being cheap, if I want to indulge that." When in the winter of 1923–24 he needed money, concentrated on producing commercial stories for *Hearst's International*, and made $17,000, he wrote Edmund Wilson that "it was all trash, and it nearly broke my heart." But he also had another way of imagining himself: "I'm a workman of letters, a professional," he would say in this mood, "I know when to write and when to stop writing." He wanted to be both a good writer and a popular one. His high living, he knew, depended on magazine money and it is significant that he devoted most of his time to short fiction during those years between 1926 and 1931 when his life became most disordered and the completion of a new novel came hard. Yet he thought of himself most proudly as a novelist. His most poignant confession of a failure to be true

24

to his talent he expressed to his daughter six months before he died: "Doubt and worry — you are as crippled by them as I am by my inability to handle money or my self-indulgences of the past. . . . What little I've accomplished has been by the most laborious and uphill work, and I wish now I'd *never* relaxed or looked back — but said at the end of *The Great Gatsby*: 'I've found my line — from now on this comes first. This is my immediate duty — without this I am nothing.'"

But the final record shows that he wrote four complete novels and more than 150 short stories. Forty-six of them he chose to print in four separate collections. In an ambitious set of plans for future productions that he once projected, there were to be in his collected works seven novels and also seven volumes of short stories. He was quite aware of his achievements as a short story writer, and twentieth-century American writing would be much poorer if it lacked six, at least, of Fitzgerald stories which are brilliant, and perhaps thirty to forty more which are full of finely observed life.

The first collection of Fitzgerald's stories in 1921 was timed by Scribner's to profit from the vogue of *This Side of Paradise*. It was called *Flappers and Philosophers*. A second collection, *Tales of the Jazz Age*, was published a year later in the wake of his second novel, *The Beautiful and Damned*. The nineteen stories in the two collections represent with more variety and perhaps more immediacy than the two first novels the manners and morals that have come to compose, at least in the minds of later historians, the Jazz Age. In 1922 we catch a glimpse of Fitzgerald imagining his relation to his Jazz Age public when he writes his editor about the second book of stories: "It will be bought by *my own personal public*, that is by the countless flappers and college kids who think I am a sort of oracle." The various mysteries that the young oracle was making known to his followers may be observed in two slight, early stories, "The Jelly-Bean," and "Bernice Bobs Her Hair." They both follow conventional formulas of popular fiction, but the young people in the stories act out a new version of the American pastoral. The man known as the Jelly-bean is a good-natured garage mechanic in a sleepy Georgia town, a son of one of the town's first families now fallen on evil days. He has been awakened to his true responsibilities in life by the kiss of a young flapper and Belle Dame sans Merci named Nancy Lamar. "With the awakening of his emotions, his first perception was a sense of futility, a dull ache at the utter grayness of his life." With this Keatsian strain life deepens for an American Jelly-bean. Nancy is the story's chief excitement. She drinks corn liquor, shoots craps with the men after a country club dance, and, in the story's best scene, wades through a pool of gasoline tapped from a car to remove a wad of chewing gum from the sole of her dancing slipper. Nancy lives with her dream of Lady Diana Manners. "Like to have boat. Like to sail out on a silver lake, say the Thames, for instance. Have champagne and caviare sandwiches along. Have about eight people." Bernice, who bobbed her hair on a dare, comes from another American Forest of Arden, Eau Claire, Wisconsin. She is an innocent who has to learn by rote a "line" for attracting boys — the same line that Fitzgerald taught his sister Annabel once when he despaired of her chances of becoming the Lady Diana Manners of St. Paul. Fitzgerald had observed two provincial societies in Montgomery, Alabama, and St. Paul, and we can watch him exploiting like a veteran novelist details of types and manners in these two stories and in "The Ice Palace." Zelda Sayre posed as the model for a southern flapper in "The Ice Palace" and Fitzgerald used their own situation to imagine the shocks that might be in store for a lively southern girl among the likable Babbitts of Minnesota. All these stories, as well as that Hollywood natural "The Off-Shore Pirate," were imagined from a young girl's dreams of a glamorous life. "Dalyrimple Goes Wrong" examines from a young ex-soldier's point of view the deceits of the world of business and politics as it is being run by a hypocritical older generation. "The Lees of Happiness" and "The Cut-Glass Bowl" imagine American domestic tragedies, lives that go down in "the flight of time and the end of beauty and unfulfilled desire." There is more pathos in these Jazz Age stories than one might expect.

Two of the stories in the first collections are important, "May Day" for what it attempts, and "The Diamond as Big as the Ritz" for what it achieves. "May Day" was probably a discarded beginning to a novel about New York. May Day 1919 was the exact day, Fitzgerald said later, when the Jazz Age began. The story is planned to carry more weight than the usual early Fitzgerald story. It uses three plots with intertwining action, like a Dos Passos chronicle novel, opens with an economic motif, the Manhattan crowds staring greedily at the glowing contents of shopwindows, and in other ways gives evidence of Fitzgerald's willingness to steal some pages from the American naturalists. The mob scenes and the two "primitives," the foot-loose soldiers looking for whiskey, may have come not from Fitzgerald's observation but from the novels of Norris and Dreiser. But if these are the story's weak spots they are also marks of its ambition. Fitzgerald wanted to use the whole loud and anarchic world of Manhattan as the background of his own forlorn state in the spring of 1919 when he was an ex-lieutenant writing advertising copy, broke, and heartsick at the loss of his girl. The portrait he draws of Gordon Sterrett, in the midst of the big money, desperately poor and depending on alcohol, shows how intensely he could project fears for his own failures — and perhaps how fascinated he would always be with the drama of failure. "I can't stand being poor," Gordon says. "You seem sort of bankrupt — morally as well as financially," says his rich Yale classmate. "Don't they usually go together?" Gordon asks. At the big dance at Delmonico's Gordon gets drunk and tells a girl how it feels to go to pieces, "Things have been snapping inside of me for four months like little hooks on a dress, and it's about to come off when a few more hooks go." Metaphors of bankruptcy and of coming unhooked are going to turn up later when Fitzgerald contemplates his own sense of failure.

"The Diamond as Big as the Ritz" is a satirical American fantasy that comes as squarely out of the bedazzled daydreams of the twenties as Hawthorne's wry fables came out of the 1840's when an earlier American generation had Utopian dreams of human nature. The young visitor to the diamond mountain kingdom, John T. Unger, from a little midwestern town named Hades, watches his host, Mr. Braddock Washington, the richest man in the world, turn at last into a madman who believes he can bribe God with his money. But young Unger has not learned much. After the diamond mountain has blown up he hates to return to his middle-class Hades with an heiress and no money. ". . . turn out your pocket and let's see what jewels you brought along. If you made a good selection we three ought to live comfortably all the rest of our lives." At the age of twenty-five Fitzgerald had written a highly imaginative folk tale of modern American life.

The Beautiful and Damned was an attempt to write a dramatic novel about a promising American life that never got anywhere; "The Flight of the Rocket," it was once called. It was the first and least convincing of what were going to be three studies of American failures. As he started the novel in August 1920, Fitzgerald wrote to his publisher that his subject was ". . . the life of Anthony Patch between his 25th and 33rd years (1913–1921). He is one of those many with the tastes and weaknesses of an artist but with no actual creative inspiration. How he and his beautiful young wife are wrecked on the shoals of dissipation is told in the story." Anthony Patch, unlike Amory Blaine, was to be placed at some distance from Fitzgerald's life. He is an American aristocrat, the only heir of a multimillionaire grandfather, "Cross" Patch, whose money goes back to the Gilded Age but whose hypocritic Puritanism is of the kind that Mencken was excoriating. Anthony's story opens as if he were going to be offered up on the smoking altars of American vulgarity and commercialism. After Harvard he spends an aesthetic year in Rome, then returns to a comfortable apartment on 52nd Street, to his small society of bachelor friends and an income of seven thousand a year left him by his mother. Anthony is not a spoiled rich boy. He is certainly not American Youth in revolt. He is simply a graceful outsider with no ambitions but to be a beleaguered gentleman, to despise his grandfather, and, he hopes, to stay unmarried.

It is hard to see where Fitzgerald is going to go with Anthony except into amiable eccentricity. He has no character except his vague cynicism, a smarting sensibility, and the seven thousand a year. But then he falls in love with Gloria Gilbert and Fitzgerald's novel begins to deepen. As a lover and a husband, and soon as a failure, inexplicable but pathetic, Anthony Patch becomes a genuine fictional character, if not a very clear one. His reality comes, as the reality of all Fitzgerald's unhappy heroes will come, out of the expression of a strong romantic will. All he has he invests in his life with Gloria. The final clue to their failure is never given us. It is not just the eternal enmity between their aspirations to beauty and the hungry generations that tread them down, though this is part of it. They live too high, waste their money, and burn themselves out. That they are simply lost from the start is almost assumed. The morning after one of their desperately drunken parties, they decide never again to give a damn, "Not to be sorry, not to loose one cry of regret, to live according to a clear code of honor toward each other, and to seek the moment's happiness as feverishly and persistently as possible." But Gloria is not enough of a Hemingway character, and Anthony is not at all one, and the code does not work. Gloria, whose conception owes something to Fitzgerald's admiration for Mencken's book on Nietzsche, begins to develop ". . . her ancient abhorrence, a conscience."

The Beautiful and Damned is a novel of mood rather than a novel of character. The misfortunes of Anthony and Gloria are forced in the plot, but the mood in places is desperate. Fitzgerald does not know what to do with his hero and heroine in the end but make them suffer. The novel will place no blame, either on the nature of things or on the injustices of society. Anthony and Gloria are finally willing to accept all the unhappy consequences as if they had earned them, but the reader has stopped believing in the logic of consequences in this novel long before. The failure of *The Beautiful and Damned* suggests where the soft spots are going to occur in Fitzgerald's art of the novel, in the presentation of character and motivation. With Anthony Patch Fitzgerald assumes that if he has displayed a man's sensibility in some detail he has achieved the study of a tragic character. The "tragedies" suffered by Anthony and Gloria, Fitzgerald's members of the lost generation, lack a moral context as the characters in *The Sun Also Rises* do not. Fitzgerald's fears of his own weaknesses and the excesses that, according to his troubled conscience, he and Zelda were learning to like too easily, endowed the parable of the Patches with moral weight and urgency for its author; but the reader had to invent the worth of the moral struggle for himself.

The Beautiful and Damned was a commercially successful novel, despite a mixed reception from reviewers. It sold 43,000 copies the first year after its serialization in the *Metropolitan Magazine*. Its success to some extent was owing to well-circulated rumors that it was autobiographical, as indeed it was in many places. Zelda Fitzgerald, in a review of the novel for the New York *Tribune*, confessed she recognized parts of her diary and some personal letters in the book. "In fact, Mr. Fitzgerald — I believe that is how he spells his name — seems to believe that plagiarism begins at home." Recognizable portraits of the Fitzgeralds appeared on the book's dust jacket. In June 1922 an essay on contemporary life in the New York *Times* recommended that remarkable book, *The Beautiful and Damned*, to anyone who wanted to understand what went on during a typical drunken party in prohibition America.

Most of Anthony and Gloria's parties occur in a cottage in Connecticut like the one the Fitzgeralds rented in Westport in May 1920 soon after their marriage. But they were too restless for suburban Connecticut and moved back to New York. In the summer of 1921 they were in England and France, and by August they had settled in St. Paul where their only child, a daughter, was born in October. They lived in St. Paul for a year after that and Fitzgerald wrote stories, began and discarded a novel with a Catholic and midwestern hero, and finished a first version of his comedy, *The Vegetable*. (It is a pretty bad play which failed on its tryout two years later.) St. Paul was too provincial for more than a short residence and by October 1922 they were living in their most memorable house, a large one in Great Neck, Long Island. One powerful image of their life on Long Island has entered American folk history through the pages in *The Great Gatsby* which describe Gatsby's parties and the people who came to them. In the Great Neck house the Fitzgeralds' life reached its expensive culmination. They spent $36,000 during their first year and then Fitzgerald wrote an essay for the *Saturday Evening Post* to show how they had done it. They entertained their literary set, which included Edmund Wilson, Ring Lardner, H. L. Mencken, and George Jean Nathan, and periodically Fitzgerald tried to stop drinking and get on with his new novel. In the spring of 1924 they decided that they must begin to save money and that the south of

France was the place to do it. By June they were established in a villa at St. Raphaël on the Riviera, and in November Fitzgerald sent the manuscript of *The Great Gatsby* off to New York. It was published in April 1925.

The Great Gatsby has been discussed and admired as much as any twentieth-century American novel, probably to the disadvantage of Fitzgerald's other fiction. None of its admirers finds it easy to explain why Fitzgerald at this point in his career should have written a novel of such perfect art — though it is usually conceded that he never reached such heights again. His discovery of Conrad and James is sometimes given credit for teaching him a new sense of proportion and control over form. But *The Great Gatsby* does so many things well that "influences" will not explain them all. The real mystery of how the novel was conceived and written may have to do with how the undisciplined life of a Long Island and St. Raphaël playboy could yield such moments of detachment and impersonality as this novel required. If we can trust Fitzgerald's backward glance from 1934 when he was writing an introduction to the Modern Library edition of *Gatsby*, it was a matter of keeping his "artistic conscience" "pure." "I had just re-read Conrad's preface to *The Nigger*, and I had recently been kidded half haywire by critics who felt that my material was such as to preclude all dealing with mature persons in a mature world." Also in 1934 he wrote his friend Bishop that he thought of *Gatsby* as his *Henry Esmond* and *Tender Is the Night* as his *Vanity Fair*: "The dramatic novel has cannons [Fitzgerald's spelling was notoriously unreliable] quite different from the philosophical, now called the psychological novel. One is a kind of *tour de force* and the other a confession of faith. It would be like comparing a sonnet sequence with an epic." Fitzgerald's language of literary sources and literary analysis always has an innocent ring. It is probably best to remember the language he used when he wrote his editor his plans for a new novel. "I want to write something *new,* something extraordinary and beautiful and simple and intricately patterned."

The Great Gatsby is worthy of all these adjectives. It was new for Fitzgerald to succeed in placing a novel of contemporary manners at such a distance from himself. Telling the story through a Conradian narrator, who was half inside and half outside the action, prevented the errors of self-identification he had fallen into with Anthony Patch. And Gatsby is not allowed to be a character who invites questions about his credibility as Anthony did. He is a figure from a romance who has wandered into a novel, the archetypal young man from the provinces who wants to become Lord Mayor, and to wake the sleeping beauty with a kiss. "Also you are right about Gatsby being blurred and patchy. I never at any one time saw him clear myself," Fitzgerald wrote a friend. But in a tour de force it is the power behind the conception that matters, and Fitzgerald was himself so sure of Gatsby's essential and primitive springs of action that he has required us to share his belief in Gatsby or reject the whole affair. "That's the whole burden of this novel," he wrote in a letter, " — the loss of those illusions that give such color to the world so that you don't care whether things are true or false as long as they partake of the magical glory."

The short novel tells the story of how James Gatz, a poor farm boy from North Dakota, imitates the example of Benjamin Franklin and other proven American moralists and rises at last to be a rich and powerful criminal named Jay Gatsby. Along the way, when he is an anonymous young lieutenant in a Kentucky training camp, when American "society" is open to him for the first time, he meets and marries in his mind, in an act of absolute commitment, a lovely southern girl named Daisy Fay. But he has to leave Daisy behind when he goes to France; and he loses her to a rich American from Chicago, Yale, and Wall Street. The only course conceivable to him when he returns is to pursue Daisy and in the

33

American way to convince her of her error, to show he is worthy of her by the only symbols available to them both, a large house with a swimming pool, dozens of silk shirts, and elaborate parties. But Daisy believes in the symbols themselves, and not in the purer reality which (for Jay Gatsby) they only faintly embody. She loses her nerve and sacrifices her lover to the world.

Gatsby's mingled dream of love and money, and the iron strength of his romantic will, make up the essence of the fable, but the art of its telling is full of astonishing tricks. To make the rise and fall of a gentleman gangster an image for the modern history of the Emersonian spirit of America was an audacious thing to attempt, but Fitzgerald got away with it. His own romantic spirit felt deeply what an Englishman has called the "myth-hunger" of Americans, our modern need to "create a manageable past out of an immense present." The poignant effect of the final, highly complex image of the novel, when Gatsby's dream and the American dream are identified, shows how deeply saturated with feeling Fitzgerald's historical imagination was. From his own American life he knew that with his generation the midwesterner had become the typical American and had returned from the old frontier to the East with a new set of dreams — about money. No reader needs to worry about Fitzgerald's complicated attraction to the glamorous rich in this novel if he puts his trust in the midwestern narrator, Nick Carraway. Nick guides us safely through all the moral confusions of the wealthy East and leads us in the end back to the provinces where the fundamental decencies depend upon a social order of families who have lived in the same house for three generations.

The success of Nick as a device for controlling the tone of the narrative is remarkable. It is the quality of his response to Gatsby that at crucial moments compels our suspension of disbelief. The tranquil tone of his recollected feelings gives the story its serenity and tempts some of its admirers to compare it to a pastoral poem. Nick is everywhere he is needed, but he never intrudes on a presented scene. He is the butt of our ironies and his own. The range of the story's ironic intentions is very wide. They encompass the wonderfully comic vulgarity of Myrtle Wilson, Tom Buchanan's mistress, as well as Daisy's almost irresistible charm. Fitzgerald's imagination plays with wit and perfect taste over the suggestive details of the story's surface: cuff buttons, a supper of cold chicken and two bottles of ale, Gatsby's shirts, and the names of the people who came to his parties. The whole novel is an imaginative feat that managed to get down the sensational display of postwar America's big money, and to include moral instructions on how to count the cost of it all. *The Great Gatsby* has by this time entered into the national literary mind as only some seemingly effortless works of the imagination can. We can see better now than even some of Fitzgerald's appreciative first reviewers that he had seized upon an important set of symbols for showing that time had run out for one image of the American ego. Poor Gatsby had been, in the novel's terms, deceived into an ignorance of his real greatness by the American world that had for its great men Tom Buchanan and Meyer Wolfsheim, the Wall Street millionaire and his colleague the racketeer. The story does not pretend to know more than this, that Americans will all be the poorer for the profanation and the loss of Gatsby's deluded imagination.

The principal fact in Fitzgerald's life between his twenty-eighth and thirty-fourth year was his inability to write a new novel. He seems to have known all along the kind of novel he wanted to write: in his terms it was to be the "philosophical, now called the psychological novel." He began a novel called *The World's Fair*, and in 1929 when he abandoned it he had written over twenty thousand words in the history of a failed life quite different from Gatsby's.

The new hero was to be a bright young movie-maker named Francis Melarky who comes to the Riviera on a vacation from Hollywood and there in a fit of anger murders his possessive mother. "In a certain sense my plot is not unlike Dreiser's in the American Tragedy," he told his editor Perkins. In 1929 he dropped the matricide plot, and changed his title to *The Drunkard's Holiday*. Then after Zelda became psychotic in 1930 he had a different kind of American tragedy to put at the center. The new novel, like *The Beautiful and Damned*, was to arise out of his own life. The pathos inherent in these years is that he seemed fated to create his own agony, and study it as if it wasn't his, before he could use it in the confessional novel he felt driven to write. Looking back on his life near the end of it, he saw what he had done and wrote to his daughter, then a freshman at Vassar, the coolest summation of the Fitzgerald legend ever made: "I am not a great man but sometimes I think the impersonal and objective quality of my talent and the sacrifices of it, in pieces, to preserve its essential value has some sort of epic grandeur. Anyhow after hours I nurse myself with delusions of that sort."

If we can accept Fitzgerald's self-analysis it only remains to be astonished at the terrible cost of preserving the "essential value" of his literary talent. Between the publication of *Gatsby* and the final return to America in 1931 the Fitzgeralds moved between Europe and America as if they could not find a home anywhere. In the south of France or in Paris Fitzgerald had even less control over his extravagance than he had in America. The sales of *Gatsby* were not up to the sales of his first two novels, but stage and screen rights brought him over $30,000. Despite yearly incomes that were always over $20,000 and often nearly $30,000, Fitzgerald came home in 1931 with hardly any money. These are the years of the steady production of magazine fiction and articles. Between 1925 and 1932 he published fifty-six stories, most of them in the *Saturday*

Evening Post. But, as Malcolm Cowley has said, the critics did not read the *Post*, and Fitzgerald's reputation began the decline from which it never recovered in his lifetime.

The best stories of those years he selected for two collections, *All the Sad Young Men*, 1926, and *Taps at Reveille*, 1935. Two recently published collections, *The Stories of F. Scott Fitzgerald*, edited by Malcolm Cowley, and *Afternoon of an Author*, edited by Arthur Mizener, have assured the modern availability of all the good magazine fiction of Fitzgerald's last fifteen years. One of the best stories in *All the Sad Young Men* is "Winter Dreams," a Jay Gatsby-Daisy Buchanan story set in St. Paul and told as if this time Gatsby had wisely given up the enchantress and learned to settle for less. But Dexter Green's dreams, like Gatsby's, are more powerful than he knows. With their loss he has lost his capacity to love anything, or even to feel anything strongly again. "Absolution" is another early story which owes its strength to the conception of Gatsby. It is a provocative sketch of the boyhood days of James Gatz in the Red River Valley of North Dakota. Fitzgerald published it as a separate story after he decided to preserve the mystery of Gatsby's early years. "The Rich Boy," written in 1926, is by common consent one of the half-dozen best Fitzgerald stories. Anson Hunter's privileged New York world is solidly established because Fitzgerald seems so intent on understanding it. The concentration of good American material in this thirty-page story might have provided a lesser novelist — provided he could have understood Anson Hunter — with the substance of a full-length fiction. The story's success seems to justify Fitzgerald's interest in the lives of the rich. He once underlined for his Hollywood friend, Sheilah Graham, a sentence from an Arnold essay, "The question, *how to live*, is itself a moral idea," and in the margin he commented, "This is Arnold at his best, absolutely without preachment." It is entirely appropriate to associate Arnold's Victorian moral seriousness with the quality of Fitzgerald's mind when he wrote "The Rich Boy."

During three years beginning in 1928 he sent the *Saturday Evening Post* a series of fourteen stories out of his boyhood and young manhood. The first eight were based on a portrait of himself as Basil Duke Lee. The last six were built around Josephine, the portrait of the magnetic seventeen-year-old girl of his first love affair. It was characteristic of Fitzgerald to relive his youth during the frustrated and unhappy days of his early thirties. His characters always know how much of their most private emotional life depends upon what Anson Hunter calls the "brightest, freshest rarest hours" which protect "that superiority he cherished in his heart." Fitzgerald was becoming acquainted with real despondency. His inability to write serious fiction sent him into desperate moods and touched off public acts of violence that ended in nights in jail. In 1928 he wrote Perkins from France, "If you see anyone I know tell 'em I hate 'em all, him especially. Never want to see 'em again. Why shouldn't I go crazy? My father is a moron and my mother is a neurotic, half insane with pathological nervous worry. Between them they haven't and never have had the brains of Calvin Coolidge. If I knew anything I'd be the best writer in America."

What he knew was his own divided life, and after Zelda's breakdown he began to write the stories of self-appraisal and self-accusation that led up to *Tender Is the Night.* In the autumn of 1930 the *Post* published the first of them, "One Trip Abroad," a Jamesian fable of the deterioration of two American innocents in Europe. Fitzgerald once wrote in his notebook, "France was a land, England was a people, but America . . . was a willingness of the heart." Nelson and Nicole Kelly come to Europe with money, a pair of small talents, his for painting, hers for singing, and the naive hope that they will find somewhere the good life. But willingness of the heart is not enough. They are not serious and self-sufficient, their

American vitality makes them restless, and they become dependent on people, parties, and alcohol. Their first sensitiveness to each other hardens into occasional violence, and they end up in the sanatoriums and rest hotels of Switzerland, "a country where very few things begin, but many things end." A better story, "Babylon Revisited" is a compassionate but morally strict portrait of a reformed American drunk who has to confront his complicity in his wife's death during a quarrel in Paris some years before. He wants desperately to get back his young daughter from her aunt and uncle's care, and he would give anything to "jump back a whole generation and trust in character again. . . ." But Charlie Wales cannot escape the furies from his past. He can only learn to face them with personal dignity.

Fitzgerald's big novel *Tender Is the Night* was written in its final form while Fitzgerald was living very close to his wife's illness. She was being treated by doctors in Baltimore — and writing her novel, *Save Me the Waltz*, to tell her version of their lives — and Fitzgerald and their daughter were making a home for her to return to in the countryside nearby. During 1932 and 1933 her health seemed to improve and he finished the manuscript. Then, early in 1934 when he was reading proofs of the novel, she had her most severe breakdown, and for the next six years, except for short periods of stability, she lived her life in hospitals. Their life together was over. It is astonishing that, written under such emotional pressures, *Tender Is the Night* is such a wise and objective novel as it is.

On the simplest level, it is the story of an American marriage. Dr. Richard Diver, a young American psychiatrist, practicing in Switzerland in 1919, falls in love with his patient, Nicole Warren of Chicago, knowing quite well that her transference to him is part of the pattern of her schizophrenia. By consecrating — to use Fitzgerald's word — himself to their marriage, she is finally cured but he is ruined. To imagine Nicole, Fitzgerald could start from Zelda in her illness and partial recovery. But his heroine is also depicted as a beautiful princess of a reigning American family, whose wealth is the source of a monstrous arrogance: Nicole's trauma was the result of her father's incestuous attack on her. Dick Diver is stigmatized with Fitzgerald's understanding of his own weaknesses. He suffers a kind of moral schizophrenia, for his precarious balance comes to depend on Nicole's need for him. After his morale has cracked he still tries to play the role of a confident man, and out of sheer emotional exhaustion he fades at last into the tender night, where he hopes nothing will ever be required of him again.

A weakness charged against the novel by some readers is that the causes of Dick Diver's deterioration are left unclear. Was it the careless, rich Nicole Warren who destroyed him, or his own bad judgment in choosing her? The only explanation the novel offers is Dick's willful self-sacrifice: he gave more generously of himself than any man could afford to. One of the reasons Dick is not coherent is that the quality of his devotion to Nicole — "a wild submergence of the soul, a dipping of all colors into an obscuring dye," it is called — is of the same degree of abandonment as Gatsby's devotion to Daisy. But Dick's romantic soul must be understood "psychologically" as Gatsby's did not need to be; the complexity of the task Fitzgerald set himself is one source of the novel's weakness. Another is Fitzgerald's use of the young movie star, Rosemary Hoyt, as the novel's Nick Carraway. Through her impressionable eyes we first see the Divers and their circle on the summer Riviera before we know the history of the marriage. To begin this long novel dramatically, as he had *Gatsby*, yields some exciting results, but Fitzgerald came to believe it was a mistake not to tell the events of the story chronologically. *Tender Is the Night* has had recent printings in both versions. Fitzgerald's readers can decide for themselves.

40

Notwithstanding these faults, *Tender Is the Night* is Fitzgerald's weightiest novel. It is full of scenes that stay alive with each rereading, the cast of characters is the largest he ever collected, and the awareness of human variety in the novel's middle distance gives it a place among those American novels which attempt the full narrative mode. Arnold's assumption that how to live is itself a moral idea provides the central substance of the novel. The society Dick has chosen is a lost one, but Dick must function as if he is not lost. To bring happiness to people, including his wife, is to help them fight back selfishness and egotism, to allow their human imaginations to function. To fill in the background of a leisured class with human dignity does not seem a futile mission to Dr. Diver until he fails. For Fitzgerald's hero "charm always had an independent existence"; he calls it "courageous grace." A life of vital response is the only version of the moral life Fitzgerald could imagine, and when Dr. Diver hears the "interior laughter" begin at the expense of his human decency he walks away. He returns to America and his life fades away in small towns in upstate New York as he tries unsuccessfully to practice medicine again.

Dick Diver is Fitzgerald's imagination of himself bereft of vitality, but also without his one strength of purpose, his devotion to literature. The poor reception of *Tender Is the Night* was a stiff blow to his confidence in himself as a writer when that confidence was about all he had left. Nearly all the influential critics discovered the same fault in the novel, that Fitzgerald was uncertain, and in the end unconvincing, about why Dick Diver fell to pieces. Fitzgerald could only fight back in letters to his friends by asking for a closer reading of his complex story. The novel sold 13,000 copies. His short stories in *Taps at Reveille*, the next year, were greeted by even more hostile reviews and the volume sold only a few thousand. For a writer who in 1925 had received letters of congratulation from Edith Wharton, T. S. Eliot, and Willa Cather, it was depressing to realize that during 1932 and 1933, while he was writing *Tender Is the Night*, the royalties paid for all his previous writing had totaled only fifty dollars. His indebtedness to his agent and his publisher began to grow as the prices paid for his stories went down. And between 1934 and 1937 his daily life declined into the crippled state that is now known after his own description of it as "the crack-up." He first fell ill with tuberculosis, and then began to give in more frequently than ever before to alcohol and despondency. Twice before his fortieth birthday he attempted suicide. By 1937 at the age of forty-one he had recovered control sufficiently to accept a writing contract in Hollywood where he could begin to pay off his debts which by this time had grown to $40,000.

Fitzgerald's public analysis of his desperate condition, published in three essays in *Esquire* in the spring of 1936, will be read differently by different people. But some kind of public penance was probably a necessary part of the pattern of Fitzgerald's life. "You've got to sell your heart," he advised a young writer in 1938, and he had — from his first college writing to *Tender Is the Night*. "Forget your personal tragedy . . ." Hemingway wrote him in 1934 after reading *Tender Is the Night*. "You see, Bo, you're not a tragic character. Neither am I. All we are is writers and what we should do is write." Hemingway and Edmund Wilson both disapproved of Fitzgerald's confessions as bad strategy for a writer. The only explanation one can imagine Fitzgerald making to them is Gatsby's explanation, that it was only personal.

The crack-up essays have become classics, as well known as the best of Fitzgerald's short fiction. The spiritual lassitude they describe is attributed to the same "lesion of vitality" and "emotional bankruptcy" that Dick Diver and Anthony Patch and all Fitzgerald's sad young men suffer. Fitzgerald calls it becoming "identified with the objects of my horror and compassion." As Fitzgerald describes it here it closely resembles what in Coleridge's ode "Dejection" is called simply the loss of joy. The process of its withdrawal from Coleridge as a power which he had drawn on too often he describes as stealing "From my own nature all the natural man." Fitzgerald was conscious of his relation to the English Romantics in his confession. He calls up the examples of Wordsworth and Keats to represent good writers who fought their way through the horrors of their lives. The loss of his natural human pieties that Fitzgerald felt he associated with a memory of "the beady-eyed men I used to see on the commuting train from Great Neck fifteen years back — men who didn't care whether the world tumbled into chaos tomorrow if it spared their houses." Fitzgerald's style was never more gracefully colloquial or his metaphors more natural and easy than in these *Esquire* pieces. "I was impelled to think. God, was it difficult! The moving about of great secret trunks." The grace of the prose has made some readers suspect that Fitzgerald is withholding the real ugliness of the experience, that he is simply imitating the gracefully guilty man in order to avoid the deeper confrontation of horror. But his language often rises above sentiment and pathos to the pure candor of a generous man who decided "There was to be no more giving of myself" and then, in writing it down, tried to give once more.

Once settled in Hollywood and in love with Miss Graham Fitzgerald returned to the East only occasionally — and usually disastrously. He needed any strength he could muster to try to stay away from drinking and hold on to his contract as a movie writer. For a year and a half he commanded a salary of over a thousand dollars a week, and, given the breaks, he said, he could double that within two years. One of his breaks was Miss Graham, who helped him to live a quiet productive life for almost a year after they met. But late in 1938 his contract was not renewed and in February 1939 he drank himself out of a movie job in Hanover, New Hampshire, a disaster that Budd Schulberg has turned into a novel and a play, *The Disenchanted.* For several months in 1939 he was in a New York hospital but by July he was writing short stories again for *Esquire.* He wrote in all twenty-two stories in the eighteen months remaining to him, seventeen of them neat and comic little stories about a corrupt movie writer named Pat Hobby, and one little masterpiece, "The Lost Decade," a sardonic picture of a talented man who had been drunk for ten years.

During the last year of his life Fitzgerald wrote as hard as his depleted capacities allowed him on the novel he left half-finished at his death, *The Last Tycoon.* It is an impressive fragment. When it was published in 1941 many of Fitzgerald's literary contemporaries, including John Dos Passos and Edmund Wilson, called it the mature fulfillment of Fitzgerald's great talent, and a belated revaluation of Fitzgerald as a writer began.

The Last Tycoon had the mark of the thirties on it as surely as his early novels had the American boom as their principal theme. The subject was Hollywood as an industry and a society, but also as an American microcosm. Instead of drawing a deft impression of American society as he had in his earlier fiction, Fitzgerald now wanted to record it. The first hundred pages of the novel take us behind the doors of studios and executive offices in Hollywood with the authority of first-rate history. The history fastens on the last of the American barons, Hollywood's top producer, Monroe Stahr, and we watch him rule a complex industry and produce a powerful popular art form with such a dedication of intelligence and will that he becomes a symbol for a vanishing American grandeur of character and role. "Unlike *Tender Is the Night,*" Fitzgerald explained, "it is not the story of deterioration — it is not depressing and not morbid in spite of the tragic ending. If one book could ever be 'like' another, I should say it is more 'like' *The Great Gatsby* . . ." The plot was to show Stahr's fight for the

cause of the powerful and responsible individual against Hollywood's labor gangsters and Communist writers. Violent action and
melodrama were to carry the story, like a Dickens novel, to seats of
power in Washington and New York. "Action is character," Fitzgerald reminded himself in one of his last notes on his novel's
progress. The action is brilliantly conceived and economically ex-
ecuted. Fitzgerald's style is lean and clear. His power of letting
his meanings emerge from incident was never more sharply displayed. At the center of his hero's last two years of life is an ill-
starred love affair, like Fitzgerald's own, that comes too late and
only reminds him of his lost first wife. But Fitzgerald kept his romantic ego in check in imagining Stahr. What obviously fascinated
him was the creation of an American type upon whom responsibility and power had descended and who was committed to build-
ing something with his power, something that would last, even
though it was only a brief scene in a movie.

It was an ironic and courageous image for Fitzgerald to cherish
in the last days of his crippled life. He had not written order into
his life, though he once noted wryly that he sometimes read his own
books for advice. But his devotion to his writing up to the end
shows how much his work flowed from his character as well as from
his talent. It is hard in coming to terms with Fitzgerald to follow
Lawrence's advice and learn to trust the tale, not the author. But
if we succeed we shall learn that the aspects of himself that he
continually made into the characters in his fiction are imaginatively
re-created American lives. He often wrote that high order of self-
revelation that reveals humanity.

◢ Selected Bibliography

Works of F. Scott Fitzgerald

This Side of Paradise. New York: Scribner's, 1920.

Flappers and Philosophers. New York: Scribner's, 1921. (Contains "The Offshore Pirate," "The Ice Palace," "Head and Shoulders," "The Cut-Glass Bowl," "Bernice Bobs Her Hair," "Benediction," "Dalyrimple Goes Wrong," and "The Four Fists.")

The Beautiful and Damned. New York: Scribner's, 1922.

Tales of the Jazz Age. New York: Scribner's, 1922. (Contains "The Jelly-Bean," "The Camel's Back," "May Day," "Porcelain and Pink," "The Diamond as Big as the Ritz," "The Curious Case of Benjamin Button," "Tarquin of Cheapside," "O Russet Witch!" "The Lees of Happiness," "Mr. Icky," and "Jemina.")

The Vegetable, or From President to Postman. New York: Scribner's, 1923.

The Great Gatsby. New York: Scribner's, 1925.

All the Sad Young Men. New York: Scribner's, 1926. (Contains "The Rich Boy," "Winter Dreams," "The Baby Party," "Absolution," "Rags Martin-Jones and the Pr–nce of W–les," "The Adjuster," "Hot and Cold Blood," "The Sensible Thing," and "Gretchen's Forty Winks.")

Tender Is the Night. New York: Scribner's, 1934.

Taps at Reveille. New York: Scribner's, 1935. (Contains Basil: 1. "The Scandal Detectives," 2. "The Freshest Boy," 3. "He Thinks He's Wonderful," 4. "The Captured Shadow," 5. "The Perfect Life"; Josephine: 1. "First Blood," 2. "A Nice Quiet Place," 3. "A Woman with a Past"; and "Crazy Sunday," "Two Wrongs," "The Night of Chancellorsville," "The Last of the Belles," "Majesty," "Family in the Wind," "A Short Trip Home," "One Interne," "The Fiend," and "Babylon Revisited.")

The Last Tycoon, edited by Edmund Wilson. New York: Scribner's, 1941.

The Crack-Up, edited by Edmund Wilson. New York: New Directions, 1945. (Contains "Echoes of the Jazz Age," "My Lost City," "Ring," "'Show Mr. and Mrs. F. to Number_____,'" "Auction—Model 1934," "Sleeping and Waking," "The Crack-Up," "Handle with Care," "Pasting It Together," "Early Success," "The Note-Books," Letters.)

The Stories of F. Scott Fitzgerald, a selection of 28 stories with an Introduction by Malcolm Cowley. New York: Scribner's, 1951. (Contains eighteen stories from the four earlier volumes and "Magnetism," "The Rough Crossing," "The Bridal Party," "An Alcoholic Case," "The Long Way Out," "Financing Finnegan," "Pat Hobby Himself: A Patriotic Short, Two Old Timers," "Three Hours between Planes," and "The Lost Decade," all previously uncollected.)

46

Afternoon of an Author; A Selection of Uncollected Stories and Essays, with an Introduction and Notes by Arthur Mizener. New York: Scribner's, 1958. (Contains twelve stories and eight essays: "A Night at the Fair," "Forging Ahead," "Basil and Cleopatra," "Outside the Cabinet-Maker's," "One Trip Abroad," "I Didn't Get Over," "Afternoon of an Author," "Design in Plaster," Pat Hobby: 1. "Boil Some Water — Lots of It," 2. "Teamed with Genius," 3. "No Harm Trying," "News of Paris — Fifteen Years Ago," "Princeton," "Who's Who — and Why," "How to Live on $36,000 a Year," "How to Live on Practically Nothing a Year," "How to Waste Material: A Note on My Generation," "Ten Years in the Advertising Business," "One Hundred False Starts," and "Author's House.")

Current American Reprints

Scribner's has reprinted all of Fitzgerald's novels in a uniform hard-cover edition (*Tender Is the Night* is printed in the revised form). It has also made available new editions of *Flappers and Philosophers,* with an Introduction by Arthur Mizener (1959), and *Taps at Reveille* (1960). *Six Tales of the Jazz Age and Other Stories,* with an Introduction by Frances Fitzgerald Lanahan (1960), contains six stories from *Tales of the Jazz Age* and three from *All the Sad Young Men.*

Three Novels of F. Scott Fitzgerald: The Great Gatsby with an Introduction by Malcolm Cowley; *Tender Is the Night* (with the Author's Final Revisions), edited by Malcolm Cowley; *The Last Tycoon, An Unfinished Novel,* edited by Edmund Wilson. New York: Scribner's Modern Standard Authors. $3.00.

Babylon Revisited and Other Stories. New York: Scribner Library. $1.25. (Contains "The Ice Palace," "May Day," "The Diamond as Big as the Ritz," "The Rich Boy," "Winter Dreams," "Absolution," "The Freshest Boy," "Crazy Sunday," "Babylon Revisited," and "The Long Way Out.")

The Crack-Up. New York: New Directions Paperbook. $1.45.

The Great Gatsby. New York: Scribner Library. $1.25.

Tender Is the Night. New York: Scribner Library. $1.45.

Bibliographies

Beebe, Maurice, and Jackson R. Bryer. "Criticism of F. Scott Fitzgerald: A Selected Checklist," *Modern Fiction Studies,* 7:82–94 (Spring 1961).

Mizener, Arthur. "Fitzgerald's Published Work," *The Far Side of Paradise.* Boston: Houghton Mifflin, 1951.

Critical and Biographical Studies

Graham, Sheilah, and Gerold Frank. *Beloved Infidel.* New York: Henry Holt, 1958. (Pp. 173–338.)

Kazin, Alfred, ed. *F. Scott Fitzgerald: The Man and His Work.* Cleveland: World, 1951.

Miller, James E., Jr. *The Fictional Technique of Scott Fitzgerald.* International Scholars Forum, vol. 9. The Hague: Martinus Nijhoff, 1957.

Mizener, Arthur. *The Far Side of Paradise.* Boston: Houghton Mifflin, 1951. Paperback edition, New York: Vintage.

Turnbull, Andrew. *Scott Fitzgerald at La Paix.* Cambridge, Mass.: Institute of Technology Publications in the Humanities, No. 22. 1956. (Reprinted from the *New Yorker*, April 7, 1956, and November 17, 1956.)

Articles and Chapters of Critical Studies

Barrett, William. "Fitzgerald and America," *Partisan Review,* 18:345–53 (May–June 1951).

Bewley, Marius. "Scott Fitzgerald and the Collapse of the American Dream," in *The Eccentric Design: Form in the Classic American Novel.* New York: Columbia University Press, 1959.

Bishop, John Peale. "The Missing All," *Virginia Quarterly Review,* 13:107–21 (Winter 1937).

Bruccoli, Matthew J., ed. *Fitzgerald Newsletter.* Number 1 (Spring 1958) through Number 11 (Fall 1960), and continuing.

Chase, Richard. *The American Novel and Its Tradition.* Garden City, N.Y.: Doubleday Anchor, 1957. Pp. 162–67.

Geismar, Maxwell. "F. Scott Fitzgerald: Orestes at the Ritz," in *The Last of the Provincials: The American Novel, 1915–1925.* Boston: Houghton Mifflin, 1943.

Harding, D. W. "Scott Fitzgerald," *Scrutiny,* 18:166–74 (Winter 1951–52).

Hoffman, Frederick J. "Points of Moral Reference: A Comparative Study of Edith Wharton and F. Scott Fitzgerald," in *English Institute Essays* 1949, edited by Alan Downer. New York: Columbia University Press, 1950.

Kuehl, John. "Scott Fitzgerald's Reading," *Princeton University Library Chronicle,* 22:58–89 (Winter 1961).

Leighton, Lawrence. "An Autopsy and a Prescription," *Hound and Horn,* 5:519–39 (July 1932).

Modern Fiction Studies, vol. 7 (Spring 1961). Essays on Fitzgerald by A. E. Dyson, Eugene White, Donald A. Yates, Matthew J. Bruccoli, Kent and Gretchen Kreuter, Robert F. McDonnell, John E. Hart, and John Kuehl.

Morris, Wright. "The Function of Nostalgia — F. Scott Fitzgerald," in *The Territory Ahead.* New York: Harcourt, Brace, 1958.

Piper, Henry Dan. "Frank Norris and Scott Fitzgerald," *Huntington Library Quarterly,* 19:393–400 (August 1956).

Schulberg, Budd. "Old Scott: The Mask, the Myth, and the Man," *Esquire,* 55:96–101 (January 1961).